ONCE UPON A RHYME

Young Writers 2004 POETRY COMPETITION

IMAGINATION FOR A NEW GENERATION

Co Durham Vol II
Edited by Sarah Marshall

First published in Great Britain in 2004 by:
Young Writers
Remus House
Coltsfoot Drive
Peterborough
PE2 9JX
Telephone: 01733 890066
Website: www.youngwriters.co.uk

All Rights Reserved

© *Copyright Contributors 2004*

SB ISBN 1 84460 562 0

Foreword

Young Writers was established in 1991 and has been passionately devoted to the promotion of reading and writing in children and young adults ever since. The quest continues today. Young Writers remains as committed to engendering the fostering of burgeoning poetic and literary talent as ever.

This year's Young Writers competition has proven as vibrant and dynamic as ever and we are delighted to present a showcase of the best poetry from across the UK. Each poem has been carefully selected from a wealth of *Once Upon A Rhyme* entries before ultimately being published in this, our twelfth primary school poetry series.

Once again, we have been supremely impressed by the overall high quality of the entries we have received. The imagination, energy and creativity which has gone into each young writer's entry made choosing the best poems a challenging and often difficult but ultimately hugely rewarding task - the general high standard of the work submitted amply vindicating this opportunity to bring their poetry to a larger appreciative audience.

We sincerely hope you are pleased with our final selection and that you will enjoy *Once Upon A Rhyme Co Durham Vol II* for many years to come.

Contents

Greenland Junior School

Sarah Hemmingway (10)	1
Simon Cowell (10)	2
Jamie Caisley (10)	3
Alex Jobson (9)	4
Katie Brown (10)	5
Christopher Graham (9)	6
Roshni Miah (10)	7
Rachel Coram (10)	8
Kerri Price (10)	9
Emily Thynne (10)	10
Jordan Smith (10)	11
Aaron Cuthbertson (10)	12
Tiffany Hogarth (10)	13
Dominic Donkin (10)	14
Liam Bell (10)	15
Elisabeth Bagnall (10)	16
Nicole Elliott (10)	17
Josh Logan (9)	18
Amy Halliday (10)	19
Tamara Brown (10)	20
Kurt Travers (10)	21
Natasha Marshall (10)	22
Jade Sutton (9)	23
Harley Hannah Robinson (10)	24
Jay Maunder (10)	25
Tiffany Morris (9)	26
Scott Luke (9)	27
Vicky Wears (10)	28
Jennifer Brown (10)	29
Fern Sarah Coulson	30
Joanne Hodgson (10)	31
Jack Austin (10)	32
Tamsyn Luke (10)	33
Janine Smith (10)	34
Raigan Taylor (10)	35

Leadgate Junior School
   Zoë Triston (9)   36
   Zoe Thompson (9)   37
   Olivia McAdam (9)   38
   Thomas Graham (10)   39
   Lauren Cranney (10)   40
   Jessica Curry (9)   41
   Leah Huscroft & Toni Bibby (9)   42
   Ben Haigh (11)   43
   Jacqueline Pigford (11)   44

Montalbo Primary School
   Joseph Jones (11)   45
   Cameron Wilkes (10)   46
   Sean Hockney (10)   47
   Hope Jevons (10)   48
   Ciaran Rowe (10)   49
   Rebecca Steen (10)   50
   Lauren Dean (10)   51
   Peter William Hartley (10)   52
   Sophie Howson (10)   53
   Lorna White (11)   54
   Adam Kicks (10)   55
   Jonathan Coll (10)   56
   Rachel Barwick (11)   57
   Matthew Allison (11)   58
   Laura Oates (10)   59
   Charlotte Holmes (10)   60
   Cameron Lawson (10)   61
   Daniel Tuck (11)   62

St Chad's RCVA School, Bishop Auckland
   Lucy Dixon (10)   63
   Emma Louise Barker (11)   64
   Daniel Potts (10)   65
   Matthew Jackson (10)   66
   Noel Oliver (10)   67
   Beth Cummins (11)   68
   Samantha Hannon (11)   69
   Daniel Edmundson (11)   70

Jake Middlemas (10)	71
Kiara Jervis (10)	72
Josh Teasdale (9)	73
Michael Turner (10)	74

St Godric's RCVA Primary School, Wheatley Hill

Ryan Jolly (9)	75
Dillon Carr (11)	76
Kurt Revitt (10)	77
Lauren Bell (10)	78
Adam Stokoe (10)	79
Emma Dixon (11)	80
Laura Coxon (11)	81
Felicity Myles (10)	82
Bethan Bradley (11)	83
Jenna Hall (10)	84
Shaun Jackson (10)	85
Olivia Jackson (9)	86
Sam Laverick (10)	87
Sophie Lenehan (10)	88
Rebecca Stephenson (11)	89
Liam Harker (11)	90
Megan Carter (10)	91
Sam Hill (9)	92
Jade Sheavills (11)	93

St Wilfrid's RCVA Primary School, Bishop Auckland

Ciaran Donnely (9)	94
Amy Bartley (8)	95
Moses Ralph (9)	96
Patrick Bentley (9)	97
Mark Dowson (9)	98
Rebecca Hutchinson (8)	99
Samantha Davey (9)	100
Alice Byrne (9)	101
Amy Biggins (9)	102
Daniel Igoe (8)	103
Maryanne McLeavey (9)	104
Tia Hinds (9)	105
Shannon Grady (8)	106
Jessica Barker (9)	107

Helen Watson (9) — 108
Amy Ross (9) — 109
Brogan McDonald (9) — 110
Catherine Clarke (9) — 111

Wingate Junior School
Beth Crossan (11) — 112
Gina Parkin (11) — 113
Sarah Dinsdale (9) — 114
Helen Carter (11) — 115
Christopher Wright (10) — 116
Emma Jones (11) — 117
Peter Clish (11) — 118
Robert Moore (11) — 119
Olivia Moran (9) — 120
Connor Wilkinson (9) — 121
Thomas McGlen (9) — 122
Hayley Davison (11) — 123
Sam Forster (8) — 124
Amy Cowey (11) — 125
Kieran Robson (9) — 126
Craig Turnbull (10) — 127
Danielle Rankin (10) — 128
Chelsea Rowe (10) — 129
Liam Laverick (10) — 130
James Blakelock (11) — 131
Sophie Gilroy (11) — 132
John Dowson (8) — 133
Kaycee Donnelly (8) — 134
Ben Harris (8) — 135
Sarah Owens (10) — 136
Carl Moyle (10) — 137
Wayne Bryson (11) — 138
Daniel Cowey (8) — 139
Lauren Smith (8) — 140
Ellie High (9) — 141
Kimberley Roache (8) — 142
Brittany Shaw (10) — 143
Rebecca Leonard (10) — 144
Jordan Hall (10) — 145
Liam Hanson (9) — 146

Martin Mason (9)	147
Nathan Goundry (9)	148
Erin Bellig (8)	149
Sasha Louise Darby (11)	150
Jennifer Coulson (8)	151
Luke Hanlon (11)	152
Craig Taylor (9)	153
Sarah Hall (11)	154
Jack Deluce (8)	155
Kayleigh Renwick (10)	156
Clare Armstrong (7)	157
Joshua Adam Hare (8)	158
Mathew Tuttle (8)	159
Jade Addison (10)	160
Chelsea McCann (10)	161
Rajvir Gill (10)	162
James Hughes (10)	163
Stacey Marriott (10)	164
Marley Donnelly (10)	165
Maryanne Jackson (10)	166
Amy Fulton (10)	167
Sarah Cowey (9)	168
Rebecca Dixon (9)	169
Chloe Davison (9)	170
Charlotte Unsworth (9)	171
David Wade (11)	172
Andrew Nichol (7)	173
Heather Marriott (7)	174
Danielle Ridden (9)	175
Rebecca Bailey (9)	176
Reece Devonport (8)	177
Jamie Robinson (8)	178
Alex Routledge (8)	179
Danielle Robinson (10)	180
Ryan Murphy (8)	181
Gemma Robson (9)	182
Lewis Coils (8)	183
Karl Laverick (8)	184
Callia Addison (7)	185
Amy Jill Kell (8)	186
Jake Dowson (8)	187
Charlotte Patterson (7)	188

Liam Harris (9)	189
Chelsea Jeffery (10)	190
Ruby McGlen (11)	191
Paul Atkinson (11)	192
Rebecca Siddle (8)	193
Dean Murrell (9)	194
Shannon Bracknell (8)	195
Laura Booth (9)	196
Ryan Parkin (9)	197
Jay Foster (9)	198
Stephanie Williams (11)	199

The Poems

School Is Cool!

Colourful walls
Tall halls, small rooms
Mr Hall's tools
Contest singer
Eating dinner.

Sarah Hemmingway (10)
Greenland Junior School

Nasty Sister Kennings

Woken sister
Bad vista
Nasty mood
Needs food
Really bored
Not ignored
Fat greedy
Not needy
Not fair
Doesn't care.

Simon Cowell (10)
Greenland Junior School

Scott

Little Scotty
Big botty
Footie kicker
Ball hitter
English muppet
Maths puppet
Good friend
That's the end.

Jamie Caisley (10)
Greenland Junior School

My Family

One day my mam asked my dad,
'Are you really a lad?'
My dad then asked my mam,
'Are you really a lamb?'
My gran acts like my mam,
My mam acts like my gran.
I asked my sister,
'Are you a mister?'
My dad is always mad.
My mam,
Calls herself Cam.

Alex Jobson (9)
Greenland Junior School

My Family

My mum is as lovely as lace,
My sister has terrible taste
And my dad is lovely too.
I don't want any others!
Would you?

Katie Brown (10)
Greenland Junior School

My Cat Murphy

My cat is a silly clown
All he does is frown
He plays with his mouse
On top of the couch
And doesn't know when to attack.

Christopher Graham (9)
Greenland Junior School

School Is Cool

School is cool
When you follow the rules!
Everyone says school is boring,
But in science you get to do some pouring.
Think about school
It's quite cool!

Roshni Miah (10)
Greenland Junior School

My Brother

Smelly big brother
Shouting, jumping, pushing pest,
Don't want no other.

Rachel Coram (10)
Greenland Junior School

Menorca

Sunny Spanish days
Wiggly pool, fun slides
Sunglasses we wear.

Kerri Price (10)
Greenland Junior School

My Puppy

Phoebe waddles and bites
She's supposed to be cute.
(Not actually) when she's biting me.
She's a ginger Ninja, ready to bite,
She's always in a fight.
Only nice when asleep
I suppose Phoebe is still lovely
                    (in her own way).

Emily Thynne (10)
Greenland Junior School

My Holidays

I like holidays
I'm in the pool all day
Always ends too quickly.

Jordan Smith (10)
Greenland Junior School

USA

USA's summer days
It's so hot, it's ninety degrees
Lovely warm salty seas.

Aaron Cuthbertson (10)
Greenland Junior School

Sunny Spain

Sunny Spain
Never rained
Whirly pool
Really cool
Slidy rides
Big tides
Cute bears
Everywhere.

Tiffany Hogarth (10)
Greenland Junior School

My Dog Kennings

Spotty dog
Walking log
Greedy mouth
Goes south
Big lugs
Chews rugs
Really fast
Extremely vast
Very nice
Eats mice
Scary dog
In fog.

Dominic Donkin (10)
Greenland Junior School

What Is The Wind?

The wind is God's Son in Heaven
It is a car going fast in Heaven
It is God blowing, to cool his coffee down
It is God blowing down the hose to make the water come out
It is God sneezing
It is angels blowing bubbles.

Liam Bell (10)
Greenland Junior School

The Beach

Molly went to the beach,
She had a lovely day
Molly and Milly went to the beach
On Sunday night
She went to her nan's on Tuesday
Went back on Wednesday
On Thursday she stayed at home
All day long.

Elisabeth Bagnall (10)
Greenland Junior School

The Newcastle Match

My dad caught the ball because he's really tall
He kicked it back,
Craig Bellamy got hurt, so Bobby said to my dad,
'Will you play?'
My dad jumped right onto the pitch,
He ran and never got a stitch.
He scored a goal without hitting the pole.
We won five-nil when my dad was ill
He always plays football.

Nicole Elliott (10)
Greenland Junior School

The Highwayman

T he legendary man called the Highwayman
H ow does he do it? Nobody knows!
E ngaged as a ghost.

H ow he was upset until he died and saw her in Heaven
I feel sorry for them both.
G ot a good reason to cry, it's sad
H ow could they die on the same day?
W hat I found - a statue of him.
A t his funeral the landlord came
Y et when you hear a ghostly galleon a
M an called the Highwayman comes riding past
A nd now we come to the end -
N ow what have we learned?

Josh Logan (9)
Greenland Junior School

In The Morning

Do you hear the birds sing, tweet, tweet, tweet
Under the morning sun?
Blue skies are here and
The night disappears, all under the morning sun.
In the morning, oh in the morning
It's the time when we all stop snoring.
In the morning.

Amy Halliday (10)
Greenland Junior School

Animals Are My Best Friends

A nimals are my best friends,
N obody can beat them.
I n the night cats scratch my door,
M issy is my best friend.
A nimals are my best friends,
L oving is what they do
S o I love them too.

Tamara Brown (10)
Greenland Junior School

What Is The Snow?

The snow is white and it glitters,
It is icing sugar.
It is pieces of wool dropping from the sky,
It is baby powder,
It is cotton wool.

Kurt Travers (10)
Greenland Junior School

The Moon

The moon is shining every night
I look up at the moon, the moon looks at me.
The moon is my best friend,
The moon smiles at me every night.
I look forward to seeing the moon tonight.

Natasha Marshall (10)
Greenland Junior School

Sweet And Spice

Liquorice Allsorts, jaw breakers, fizzy whips,
Chocolate sticks, flapjacks, doughnuts
Lollies, gummy bears,
Tongue tasting teasers, Highland toffee,
Chewits, sweet chews, sour chews,
Dairy Milk chocolate, Topics, slimy faces.
Crisps, flavoured pop, brain lickers, fruit flavoured pop
All in one shop.

Jade Sutton (9)
Greenland Junior School

The Highwayman

The Highwayman went clippety, clippety-clop.
Oh-oh yes, oh yes he did!
He found a carriage and went inside and took all
of the money and gold.
Oh-oh yes, oh yes he did!
He went clippety, clippety-clop found another carriage
went inside but he couldn't find any money or gold
it was empty everywhere, and he realised
he was in an empty carriage.
He went clippety, clippety-clop.
Oh-oh yes, oh yes he did!
Then he found another carriage and went inside,
he killed a person to keep that person quiet
so he got the money and the gold.
Then he went clippety, clippety-clop down the road.

Harley Hannah Robinson (10)
Greenland Junior School

Fiery Dragon

A dragon is big and fiery
It fires fire and puffs air
It flies in the air like a bird
It slopes down and it grabs its enemy
Its eyes go red when it's mad
Its claws are big and sharp
It lands on the floor and lies down like a dog.

Jay Maunder (10)
Greenland Junior School

The Sun Is Shining

The sun is shining everywhere
People playing every day,
Never raining always shining
People playing in the sea.
People having barbecues every day,
People have water fights, everywhere.
People loving the sun,
People singing on the stage.
People dancing everywhere,
People having fun every day.

Tiffany Morris (9)
Greenland Junior School

Wake Up Now!

Mum said, 'Wake up now!'
'No!'
'Yes!'
'Come on lazy, or you will be late.'
'So I'll come down in five - I hate you
So ha, ha, ha, ha, ha, ha!'

Scott Luke (9)
Greenland Junior School

Friends

All my friends care for me
We always carry on
We always play around the trees
We always have sleepovers
We will always be best friends.

Friends are there for you,
Run along the street with them.
Even when you're poorly they come.
Nice and caring they are,
Driving away, they will cry for you.

Vicky Wears (10)
Greenland Junior School

About My Family

F amily is special to us
A unties are special as well
M ums and dads love us
I t is great having a family
L ife is good, having a brother
Y ou and me are great together.

Jennifer Brown (10)
Greenland Junior School

Friends

Friends are great
They are very good mates
They are always there
And always care.

Fern Sarah Coulson
Greenland Junior School

The Sun

The sun is hot,
It always shines in the sky,
You go red if you stay out long enough,
You go brown after red,
You only get sun in the summer.

Joanne Hodgson (10)
Greenland Junior School

The Simpsons

Bart and Santa's little helper are the coolest,
Lisa is a nerd, so is Milhouse
Homer is fat, so is Barny.
Moe is funny, so is Comic Book Guy.
Marge is a worry boots,
Maggie is the smartest,
Apu is greedy for money.
Snake is a low-life
Burns is a devil,
Smithers is the Devil's helper,
The Flanders are God's goody goodies,
Lenny is drunk,
Cari is stupid.

Jack Austin (10)
Greenland Junior School

What Is The Snow?

Snow is like baby powder sprinkling down,
Snow is soft
Snow is like feathers
Snow is cold
Snow is wet
Snow is frost coming down
Snow is like flowers
Snow is just like icing
Snow is like ice cream balls
Snow is like apple inside
Snow is like white paper
Snow is like cotton wool
Snow is like sheep's fur.

Tamsyn Luke (10)
Greenland Junior School

My Pet Cats - Haiku

Dennis is greedy
Jack is older and blacker
But they are so cute.

Janine Smith (10)
Greenland Junior School

My Dog - Haiku

My dog is bonkers
It walks into walls
I give it a stroke.

Raigan Taylor (10)
Greenland Junior School

Phantom Clouds

I wandered through the forest,
I heard a gunshot crack,
Then I saw my dead body with a bullet on the forest floor,
I promised my mum not to go far. I promised.

I whisper, 'I am a phantom,'
Through the woods I go.
I sob quietly this time but longer,
I am by a canal and the reeds blow.

I see the hazy outline of other phantoms
But they don't see me.
I was angry at my killer, as angry as can be
I went back into the forest, I could hardly see.
I weep for my family.

I began to think who did it, but I couldn't think.
I wandered about and found a fellow phantom,
I asked what is our purpose. I couldn't think!

His reply was, 'My friend, we are clouds,
Lonely, forgotten, icy clouds!'

Zoë Triston (9)
Leadgate Junior School

I Don't Want . . .

I don't want a dog.
I don't want a frog.
What do you want?
I don't want anything made by you.
I don't want anything, even if you buy me two.
What do you want?
I don't want a cat.
I don't want a bat.
What do you want?
I want a friend!

Zoe Thompson (9)
Leadgate Junior School

I Have! I Have!

Have you ever seen an elephant fly?
I have, I have.
Have you ever seen the grass turn pink?
I have, I have.
Have you ever seen a flower talk?
I have, I have.
Have you ever seen the teddies come alive at night?
I have, I have.
Have you really seen these things come true?
Of course I have silly -
But only in my dreams come true!

Olivia McAdam (9)
Leadgate Junior School

A Knight's Tale

Galloping along the high road,
The strong silver figure,
With his strong shield
With his long sharp blade
And his mighty lance.
He goes searching . . .
Searching for justice, valour and love,
He lives to do his sworn duty,
He fights and slays his enemy.
He charges to the front of the battlefield,
And fights the enemy for his country
And protects the weak.
Only a few living souls become these armed men,
We offer lives to these people,
But will I become a knight?

Thomas Graham (10)
Leadgate Junior School

The Mini Bananarama!

The mini Bananarama
Crashed into a farmer.
Stole his loyal llama
The evil Bananarama!

The evil Bananarama
Hurt that joyful farmer,
Kidnapped the loyal llama
The stupid Bananarama!

The stupid Bananarama
Sailed away from the farmer,
Got sunk by the llama
The sunken Bananarama!

The sunken Bananarama,
Was laughed at by the farmer,
The crazy loyal llama,
Stayed in the Bananarama.

Then the llama died and the boat was sunk!

Lauren Cranney (10)
Leadgate Junior School

Springtime Is Here

This time of year
When flowers bloom,
The drift of fragrance
Spreads through my room.
I close my eyes
The sun so strong,
Heat and sweet smells
And a bird's sweet song.
It means Mother Nature is alive and strong.

Jessica Curry (9)
Leadgate Junior School

Dogs

It was two thousand and four
On May the twenty-sixth day.
Heaving lump in the house
'Help!' I hear you crying,
Crying for your life.

Your friend's lying hurt on the floor,
Your owner beating you with the door.
You cry more and more.

He kicks you down the tumbling stairs,
You run outside and he ties you up.
'Save me, save me!' you bark.

Save dogs!

Leah Huscroft & Toni Bibby (9)
Leadgate Junior School

Tigers

Stop killing tigers for their fur,
Stop killing tigers for their fur,
It is cruelty.

They can run as fast as a train at full
Speed
And they are a sly, mean machine.

Stop killing tigers for their fur,
Stop killing tigers for their fur,
It is cruelty.

They creep along in search of prey
When they see them he bounces and
Pounces to bring them down

Stop killing tigers for their fur,
Stop killing tigers for their fur,
It is cruelty.

Ben Haigh (11)
Leadgate Junior School

One Night

One night when I went to bed
I fell asleep and dreamt that
I saw a huge monster in my head
His head was made out of cement
His raging eyes were the colour of blood
I thought, *will he gobble me up?*
And then he said, 'I could, I would and I should!'
I woke up later that night
Because I'd had a terrible fright
I went back to sleep and
Then I saw him creep and creep.
I tossed and turned and
Whilst he roared and shouted
My tummy churned
And then he pouted
I froze . . .
And then I heard my mum say,
'Come on Jack, it's time to get up!'

Jacqueline Pigford (11)
Leadgate Junior School

Nature Is . . .

Nature is a breeze rustling through the trees,
Nature is a mountain reaching great heights.
Nature is silence by the natural spring,
Nature is a seed waiting to grow.
Nature is a path of green, leading through a forest.
Nature is a breath of fresh air by the salty sea.
Nature is an animal silently stalking its prey,
Nature is a wonderful thing.

Joseph Jones (11)
Montalbo Primary School

The Dangerous Jungle

Jungles are a dangerous place to be in.
Underneath all the moist grass lives loads of bugs.
Nearby there are lots of dangerous animals waiting for prey!
Gear you will need to survive in the deadly jungle with loads of food.
Lying right beside you, a tiger waiting for your first move!
Each animal begins to run and *snap* goes the tiger's mouth,
Snap he goes and the rabbit is dead!

Cameron Wilkes (10)
Montalbo Primary School

The Greek Gods

The Greek gods and goddesses are
Famous for different things,
Like Hermes who has wings,
Apollo who drives a chariot of fire,
Driving it higher and higher

Demeter the goddess of corn
And Pan who blows on his horn.
There's Athene the goddess of war.
To Ares who has a sword and more.

Eros who has a bow
And Poseidon in his chariot
How far can he go?
Hera the goddess of love,
Who sits on a cloud up above.

Dionysus the god of wine
To Hephaetus who makes horse shoes, size nine.
Zeus and Hades are very much brothers,
Hades is the one who kills the others.
Zeus is the king of the gods.

Sean Hockney (10)
Montalbo Primary School

What If I Could . . .

What if I could reach the rainbow
and get the pot of gold?
What if I could touch the moon and
do what I am told?

What if I could be a king and rule
a place of my own?
What if I could be a spaceman and
you'll know where I go?

What if I could be a football player
and win the World Cup?
What if I could be a baker and the
wonderful cakes I'll cook?

What if I could be an athlete
and run the Olympic race?
What if I could be an exerciser
and always keep my pace?

Hope Jevons (10)
Montalbo Primary School

My Bedroom

My bedroom is a war field
A path through the middle.
Separating two armies apart,
Gravestones for people, passed away.

Climbing on shelves to get a view
Of the army shooting you.
Then the army blows up your base
Leaving them in a state.

But so long as there is a path
For people to cross.
No one is bothered
So nobody finds out.

All the toys fight each day,
To try and get the most play.
Then they go into battle,
It's surprising, isn't it?

Ciaran Rowe (10)
Montalbo Primary School

The Wonderful Words Of Space

Space is like a giant black hole,
Space is as black as coal.
The stars drift through the sky,
Space is so high, high, high!
The darkness in space.

Space is dark like each night,
Space is too far to see in sight.
The moon gleams down,
It shines in the town,
The darkness in space.

The stars twinkle all night long,
When everybody sings a song.
Earth is like a ball,
Even though it's bigger than a mall.
The darkness in space.

Mars is far, far away,
But the stars are here today.
The moon's face is looking at you,
The moon goes in, the sun comes out too.
The darkness in space.

Rebecca Steen (10)
Montalbo Primary School

My Holiday

My holiday was strange,
Monday I woke up in a jungle,
Misty and foggy, it was lonely,
Spook. It made me frightened and scared,
My holiday was strange.

My holiday was strange,
Tuesday I woke up in a desert,
Dry and dusty by myself,
Sand, made sandstorms, no water there,
My holiday was strange.

My holiday was strange,
Wednesday I woke up in a cave,
Rocks crumble in your hands
I nearly got trapped, rock fell over the door,
My holiday was strange.

My holiday was strange,
Thursday I woke up in a castle.
Daggers and swords surround me,
Suits of armour, ready for war
My holiday was strange.

My holiday was strange,
Friday I woke up in a prison,
Cell doors, hard as iron,
I was locked in!
My holiday was strange.

Lauren Dean (10)
Montalbo Primary School

Lessons Lines

M is for multiplying which looks like this 'x',
A is for algebra addition,
T is for trying your hardest which everyone does,
H is for help which everyone gets from the teacher,
S is for SATs, subtracting and satisfying answers.

Peter William Hartley (10)
Montalbo Primary School

The Secrets Of Space

The darkness of space.

The rockets flying through the sky,
The happiness of space must never die,
Up there is the rocky moon,
Planet Mars is coming soon.

The darkness of space.

Venus, Saturn, Pluto, the sun,
The solar system is on the run,
The sun is like a great big star,
Although it won't travel far.

The darkness of space.

The Earth is like a great big ball,
Off the sides you would never fall,
The stars give a great big shine,
Although they are very fine.

The darkness of space.

The spacecrafts are very clever,
But they won't change the weather
The solar system goes around,
You could not buy it for a pound.

The darkness of space.

Sophie Howson (10)
Montalbo Primary School

The Eagle

The eagle fishes day by day,
Looking for his fishy prey.
He takes it away to his mountain home,
Where he sits and eats all alone.
The eagle fishes for his prey,
Flying, flying, day by day.
He takes it away to his mountain walls,
Before, like a bomb, he falls!

Lorna White (11)
Montalbo Primary School

Someone Special

S is for someone special just like you
P is for people just like you
E is for everyone who works like you
C is for cuddles that you give me
I is for icicles which look as beautiful as you
A is for ants that feed their young
L is for love that you give me.

M is for money that you give me
U is for umbrellas that keep us dry
M is for Mum whom I love lots.

You are my friend who keeps me safe
Oh I love you and you love me
We love each other and that is true.

Adam Kicks (10)
Montalbo Primary School

Rainforests

R is for rivers murky and infested,
A is for Amazon, bright, green and glimmering.
I is for insects patterned with great rhythm,
N is for nightfall when animals lurk and seek.
F is for flowers with many scents and colours,
O is for oranges and many wonderful fruits.
R is for rainstorms thundering and flashing,
E is for eagles ruling the Amazon,
S is for sunlight shining through the trees,
T is for thunderstorms tearing down the forest.
S is for safaris concluding this adventure.

Jonathan Coll (10)
Montalbo Primary School

15 Things I Hate About You

I hate the way you walk
And the way you talk.
I never listen.
I hate the way you talk about stuff
As you say it's lush.
I never listen.
As you say about your guitar
As well as your car
I never listen.
As you're drinking coffee
You're always thinking of toffee
I never listen.
I hate the way you look
And the way you cook.
I never listen.

Rachel Barwick (11)
Montalbo Primary School

English

E is for England,
N is for new, like lots of things are,
G is for geography, that is a subject.
L is for lessons,
I is for ink, which can leak.
S is for switches,
H is for height, as high as a skyscraper.

Matthew Allison (11)
Montalbo Primary School

You Are Special

Do not think you're not wanted
Because that won't be true.
And remember your parents love you.

You are special!

Life may not go as planned
And some things may be grand,
But you still think no one loves you.

You are special!

Maybe you get bullied
Then you think you were a mistake.

You are special!

Remember you are someone special
No matter what people say.

Laura Oates (10)
Montalbo Primary School

Sunrise

When the sun has risen
And performed a prism,
The rosebuds open with joy.

When the bluebells ring and
The birds start to sing,
The morning starts dawning and
Every living thing starts yawning
Everyone knows it's morning.

Children start skipping, birds start singing,
Church bells start ringing.
The scent of sweet blossom is blooming
And the bluebirds start tuning.

The fish start jumping high up the river.
Sticklebacks stick to an old wrecked stick.
When the river starts flowing,
Boatmen start rowing.

Dogs start barking while people start
Darting away.

Charlotte Holmes (10)
Montalbo Primary School

Perfection

P erfection cannot be given or taken, it is found through practice.
E xperience is always required to grasp perfection.
R ested on a see-saw perfection can be a good or bad thing.
F inding perfection can be easy, it can be hard.
E tiquette is needed to acquire perfection.
C alling perfection satisfaction is not always correct.
T here is a barrier between perfection and arrogance.

Cameron Lawson (10)
Montalbo Primary School

The Run

Getting ready to run, yes I know it sounds really fun,
At first lots of silence, 'It's only fun please no violence,'
As the gun went bang (I'm trying not to use any slang),
We all started to sprint at first, some people say the course is cursed,
I was doing well but the school was doing swell,
Lots of time had passed, we all felt like we'd been gassed
When we passed the finish line!

Daniel Tuck (11)
Montalbo Primary School

A Special Place At Christmas

Through a window dark but clear,
Happy now that Christmas is here.
See some carollers walking past,
Singing their hearts out, Christmas at last.
See a full moon in the sky,
Sparkling like a diamond in your eye.

Lucy Dixon (10)
St Chad's RCVA School, Bishop Auckland

What Lies Beyond My Window Frame?

Puzzled
I sit and stare
Wondering what lies beyond my window frame,
The thunderous noises of the city sound like cries of people in agony,
The city lights flash before my eyes,
My heart misses a beat as I realise the fire is rising higher,
Reaching out its warm hands trying to snatch me away -
I can feel the pain and agony of those people in the blazing hot fire,
What is going through my mind at this moment is unbearable.
I wonder what terrible things will happen next in my life.

Emma Louise Barker (11)
St Chad's RCVA School, Bishop Auckland

Castle

A man with his arms outstretched still offering protection after
                                            all these years,
His mouth still snaps shut after every sharp comment.
Eyes like window slits - barely open,
His bulbous nose fat like the end of a cannon,
His ears still flap as he picks up every comment and conversation,
Memories of yesterday still fresh in his mind.

Daniel Potts (10)
St Chad's RCVA School, Bishop Auckland

Sea Poem

The sea is not calm, like a baby asleep,
The sea is home to sparkling fish
The sea is not gentle.

The sea can be rough,
The sea can be wild,
The sea can be really tough.

The sea can be salty,
The sea can be lots of fun.

Matthew Jackson (10)
St Chad's RCVA School, Bishop Auckland

The Castle

A castle is an old woman
Whose eyes twinkle with love and care for her grandchildren,
Wearing her aqua necklace,
The stones reflect the moonlight.
The feathers on her hat flutter in the breeze like the flags on a turret.
The chains hold the drawbridge like her knitting needles hold her wool.

Noel Oliver (10)
St Chad's RCVA School, Bishop Auckland

The Old Town House

The old town house
Is a very old man
Showing off his polished boot to everyone who passes by,
His dreary eyes staring in content.

When visitors come his way
They see his face so grey.
As they walk up the stone steps,
They hear each of his unwelcoming words.

The hat he wears has turned grey and crooked with age,
He scowls, taking a large puff of his brown cigar.

Beth Cummins (11)
St Chad's RCVA School, Bishop Auckland

Night Falls

Outside night falls,
Winds whisper peacefully,
Shaggy wolves howl.

Bats glide swiftly across,
Rats scuttle across the moonlit floor,
Eyes in every direction.

Shapes are left looming
While mist starts to cover the ground,
Crawling, creepy creatures prowl.

While shadows fall,
While a full moon beams outside,
It becomes daybreak!

Samantha Hannon (11)
St Chad's RCVA School, Bishop Auckland

Number 6

Number 6 is a very old lady,
Her face is lathered in white powder.
The wrinkles on her face reveal years of laughter, also sadness.
Her heart glows like the warmth of the fire
Burning for the love of her grandson.

The windows are square just like her glasses, never replaced.
Her dress is a pattern of blooming flowers.
Her washing blows in the wind,
Like a thread of wool dangling from her wool jumper.

Daniel Edmundson (11)
St Chad's RCVA School, Bishop Auckland

Deserted House

In a deserted house totally black,
Rats chewing frantically on old, rotten chairs,
Bats flying silently in a rush,
Sit down and stare at the rattling window.
The stairs squeak deafeningly like mice.
Walk down to the basement, see the big eyes staring at you.
See the blood of a murder victim,
In the attic spiders that need a haircut
The spiders spin webs like treacle on a pancake,
They are spinning their webs like an old woman sewing.

Jake Middlemas (10)
St Chad's RCVA School, Bishop Auckland

Model Mansion

Dark brown skin with glistening sunglasses,
Ivy hair and a deep red hat,
Wearing a bright green outfit and smelling of roses,
Puffing smoke ascending into the air,
Like painted fingertips curling around a glass.
A pond-like brooch attached to her clothes,
Reflecting her status and grandeur.

Kiara Jervis (10)
St Chad's RCVA School, Bishop Auckland

Deserted House

In a deserted house pitch-black.
Rats chew on old wooden chairs.
Bats fly silently through the house never stopping.
The stairs squeak on and on like mice.
The windows rattle in the howling wind.
Books - hundreds of years old, still rotting away.
Spiders spinning their webs slowly
But, yet there are hundreds of them.
There sits an old man reading,
What is he doing here in this haunted house?
Nobody knows - do you?

Josh Teasdale (9)
St Chad's RCVA School, Bishop Auckland

The Moonlight

The moonlight glares through the dark blue sky.
Down on to the cottage roof and then back up high.
The river's dark reflections shine at night,
Through the clouds the sky beams at any sight.
Clouds drift away as morning awakes.

Michael Turner (10)
St Chad's RCVA School, Bishop Auckland

Jets

S upersonic
U nbelievable
P ower
E ngine
R oars out loud

J erks
E ventually
T wins

E choing
N oises
G rand
I nformation
N early
E xhausted

Ryan Jolly (9)
St Godric's RCVA Primary School, Wheatley Hill

Sport

Running and jumping doing lots of sports
We're playing football in the new grand hall.
We come again
We play again
Heea, heea, heea, heea
Heea, heea, heea, heea.
Swinging and whacking in the tennis court
We all bat around the balls that we found.
Heea, heea, heea, heea.

Dillon Carr (11)
St Godric's RCVA Primary School, Wheatley Hill

The War Against Hitler

The English armies are setting up
To attack the Germans
1, 2, 3, 4, 1, 2, 3, 4
Hup, two, three, four, hup, two, three, four.

The German forces are on their way
The reinforcements are far away
1, 2, 3, 4, 1, 2, 3, 4
Hup, two, three, four, hup, two, three, four.

Here comes Hitler, run away
Leave it to the general to find the way
1, 2, 3, 4, 1, 2, 3, 4
Hup, two, three, four, hup, two, three, four.

The battle is won for today
We'll have to see what happens on another day
1, 2, 3, 4, 1, 2, 3, 4
Hup, two, three, four, hup, two, three, four.

The war is over, hooray, hooray
The diplomacy has worked on this glorious day
1, 2, 3, 4, 1, 2, 3, 4
Hup, two, three, four, hup, two, three, four.

Kurt Revitt (10)
St Godric's RCVA Primary School, Wheatley Hill

Books Rule

Romantic novels are like hugging pink, fluffy pillows,
They are warm hearted and delicious,
Horror stories are like ashes from a burnt fire,
They are dark, damp and mysterious,
Humour books are like walking into a joke shop.

Books are the best
Books are the greatest
Books rule!

Harry Potter is so mind blowing,
It's crazy, it's magical, it's cheesy,
Tracy Beaker is really wild,
She thinks everything is easy-peasy,
The Lord Of The Rings is creepy, but excellent.

Books are the best
Books are the greatest
Books rule!

Some pictures are so cool,
Most pictures are colourful and jump out on you,
Some words are really funky,
Most words are really boring which doesn't help you.

Books rule!
Books rule!
What?
Books rule!

Lauren Bell (10)
St Godric's RCVA Primary School, Wheatley Hill

I Like Being A . . .

I like being a computer,
To beat my owner at games,
I give you loads of information
From around the whole nation.

I get new hardware and some software
It serves her right for spilling pop on me,
All I can type now is . . .
Silly Sally
Sloppy Sally
Stupid Sally
Broke me.

Adam Stokoe (10)
St Godric's RCVA Primary School, Wheatley Hill

Up The Attic

And something whistling
Dark, woolly hat
Black winter coats
Chewed old dog mats
Christmas tree baubles
Big Christmas tree
Good Christmas lights
Up the attic.

Emma Dixon (11)
St Godric's RCVA Primary School, Wheatley Hill

Barking Dogs

Dogs, dogs bury bones,
Dogs, dogs dig in stones,
Dogs, dogs chase cats and birds,
But dogs don't speak in English words.

Woof, woof, bark, bark, howl, howl, *grrr!*

Gundogs catch pheasants,
And bring them to you as presents,
Dogs sniff all around,
And when you're done off to the *pound!*

Woof, woof, bark, bark, howl, howl, *grrr!*

In we go whimpering and crying,
I bet they all wish they were flying,
Just so they could get out of here,
And then they would disappear.

Woof, woof, bark, bark, howl, howl, *grrr!*

Now I tell you the end of the story,
All the pound dogs are walking in glory,
Just because the pound closed down,
And now they're wild in the town.

Woof, woof, bark, bark, howl, howl, *grrr!*

Laura Coxon (11)
St Godric's RCVA Primary School, Wheatley Hill

Scribbles

Scribbles are exciting,
They're so motivating,
And that's affirmascribble.

Let me ask you now,
Are you a scribbler?
Is it yes, or no, or maybe so?

As we say hello or negascribble,
To non scribblastic things or as we
Say, scribblebye or bye-bye.

Felicity Myles (10)
St Godric's RCVA Primary School, Wheatley Hill

Summer

S unny days,
U nlimited ice lollies,
M ountains of fun,
M asses of ice cream,
E njoying the sun,
R ed-hot days don't go away.

Bethan Bradley (11)
St Godric's RCVA Primary School, Wheatley Hill

Smaug The Dragon

Smaug the dragon was big and strong,
He went to town one day.
He did not stay for very long,
And scared the folk away.

The sky lit up with burning flames,
The town was in a mess,
Smaug was playing frightful games,
And could not care less.

A man called Bard who was so smart,
Went to kill the dragon,
He shot an arrow through his heart,
With help by Bilbo Baggins.

Jenna Hall (10)
St Godric's RCVA Primary School, Wheatley Hill

The Poor Old Man From Kilkenny

There was an old man from Kilkenny
Who never spent more than a penny
He spent all that money
On onions and honey
That weird old man from Kilkenny.

Shaun Jackson (10)
St Godric's RCVA Primary School, Wheatley Hill

My Dream Holiday

Australia is my dream holiday,
I want to lie in the sand and play,
Surfing is very cool,
Because the Aussie's really rule,
The waves are crashing,
People are dashing,
The sound of the sea,
Seems loud to me,
Later this very day,
In the pool we will play,
And that is my dream holiday.

Olivia Jackson (9)
St Godric's RCVA Primary School, Wheatley Hill

There Was A Man From Baghdad

There was a man from Baghdad,
Everyone said he was mad,
Created a plane,
Became insane,
That poor old man from Baghdad.

Sam Laverick (10)
St Godric's RCVA Primary School, Wheatley Hill

Love

Love is pink
It smells like flowers,
It tastes like chocolate,
It sounds like a song,
Love feels soft and furry,
Love lives in your heart.

Sophie Lenehan (10)
St Godric's RCVA Primary School, Wheatley Hill

The Bank In The Child's View

Pulled up in the car with my mam,
Rather be buying a cola can,
Walking into the bank to pay a loan,
Rather be talking on my mobile phone.

Beep, beep, ching, ching, sounds of the bank,
Beep, beep, ching, ching, sounds of the bank.

Mam at the cashpoint withdrawing,
Rather be at home snoozing and snoring,
Dad's in the bank with his pay cheque,
Rather be playing on a game called Tic Teck.

Beep, beep, ching, ching, sounds of the bank,
Beep, beep, ching, ching, sounds of the bank.

When I get older and go to the bank,
When I ask my children if they want to come they'll say, 'No thanks,'
When I pull them into the bank to pay a loan
All they'll do is moan, moan, moan.

Moan, moan, moan!

Rebecca Stephenson (11)
St Godric's RCVA Primary School, Wheatley Hill

DRZ 450

By pulling it out,
By starting the engine,
1234, starting to go,
Spinning it around,
We hear the sound,
Of the cog grinding into gear.

1234, 1234, 1234,
1234, 1234, 1234.

Sound of the big, yellow bike roaring,
It's not boring,
I'm going for dinner,
I hope I am the winner.

1234, 1234, 1234,
1234, 1234, 1234.

I got chased into the pit,
And I nearly took a fit,
Then I went to buy my new kit,
And the kit didn't fit.

1234, 1234, 1234,
1234, 1234, 1234.

Liam Harker (11)
St Godric's RCVA Primary School, Wheatley Hill

The Bustling Streets

Running up the busy street,
Watching all the people meet.
We come again
To watch again,
Step, step, step, step stepping by,
Step, step, step, step stepping by.

Crowds of people in a hurry,
Seeing them all rush and scurry.
We come again
To watch again,
Step, step, step, step stepping by.
Step, step, step, step, stepping by.

Tall and short, thin and fat,
Wearing lots of different hats.
We come again
To watch again,
Step, step, step, step stepping by,
Step, step, step, step stepping by.

Megan Carter (10)
St Godric's RCVA Primary School, Wheatley Hill

Vehicles And Animals

C is for caterpillar,
A is for aeroplane,
R is for riddle,
S is for super!

V is for village,
A is for actor,
N is for nice,
S is for super!

C is for cow,
A is for aunt,
T is for tune,
S is for super!

C is for car,
O is for octopus,
W is for wand,
S is for super!

Sam Hill (9)
St Godric's RCVA Primary School, Wheatley Hill

The Cute Dolphin

Diving through the air
Swimming down below,
We never stop long,
We're always on the go.

Splish, splash, splosh!
Splish, splash, splosh!

Playing with our friends,
Having lots of fun,
Never ever rain,
Always in the sun.

Splish, splash, splosh!
Splish, splash, splosh!

Having lots of visitors
To watch us swim,
Sometimes they capture us
And hurt our fins.

Splish, splash, splosh!
Splish, splash, splosh!

Some days they swim with us,
They always love to play
With balls, hoops and stuff,
They're never in the way.

Splish! Splash! Splosh!
Splish! Splash! Splosh!

I love my daily fish,
I act like one myself,
Most days they're quite tasty,
They help me with my health.

Jade Sheavills (11)
St Godric's RCVA Primary School, Wheatley Hill

The Writer Of This Poem
(Based on 'The Writer Of This Poem' by Roger McGough)

The writer of this poem is as sly as a kid,
As quick as a whiz,
As thin as a stick
And as thick as a brick,
As scary as a scar,
As sharp as a knife,
As loud as a bumblebee,
As prickly as a pineapple,
As wobbly as a jelly,
As bouncy as can be
And as funny as me.

Ciaran Donnely (9)
St Wilfrid's RCVA Primary School, Bishop Auckland

Epitaphs

Here lies the body
Of the BFG
Running down a hill,
Smashed into a tree.

Here lies the body
Of Winnie the Pooh
Running all over,
He needed the loo.

Here lies the body
Of Cinderella
Who was really jealous
Of a famous fella.

Amy Bartley (8)
St Wilfrid's RCVA Primary School, Bishop Auckland

You Might . . .

You might be outside
You might be on the phone
You might be giving the dog a bone
You might be at the shop
You might be giving me a drink of pop
You might be in bed
You might be in the shed
You might be at the outlet
You might be giving the dog its tablet
But wherever you are I still love you
Because you are simply the best
Of all the rest.

Moses Ralph (9)
St Wilfrid's RCVA Primary School, Bishop Auckland

Here Lies The Body

Here lie the bodies
of the three little pigs,
pushed in boiling water
by wolves wearing wigs.

Here lies the body
of Goldilocks,
killed by the bears
when they stuffed her in a box.

Patrick Bentley (9)
St Wilfrid's RCVA Primary School, Bishop Auckland

The Writer Of This Poem
(Inspired by 'The Writer Of This Poem' by Roger McGough)

Is as skinny as a pole,
with a head like a mole.
He has a mouth like a hole.
His eyes are like coal.
He eats from a plate that looks like a bowl.
He is as messy as a monkey and as quiet as a vole.
His name is Mark and he lives in the dark.

Mark Dowson (9)
St Wilfrid's RCVA Primary School, Bishop Auckland

The Writer Of This Poem
(Based on 'The Writer Of This Poem' by Roger McGough)

The writer of this poem is as strong as an ox,
As long as a leopard,
As sharp as a fox.

As small as a mouse,
As bold as a bear,
As funny as a joke,
As sweet as a pear.

As fast as a hare,
As happy as a child,
As gusty as the wind when it is very wild.

Rebecca Hutchinson (8)
St Wilfrid's RCVA Primary School, Bishop Auckland

My Limericks

There was once a dog of Spain
who was in a lot of pain
as he lay in a tray
in the middle of May
That dog got run over by a train.

There was once a lady of France
who danced in her pants and got them in a trance
for she was so stupid
as she danced with Rupid
That dancing lady of France.

There once was a man of Chile
who wore a top that was frilly
everyone used to laugh
when he walked down the path
That frilly man of Chile.

Samantha Davey (9)
St Wilfrid's RCVA Primary School, Bishop Auckland

Christmas

Snow is falling all over the ground.
Under the tree presents can be found.
Santa's coming in his sleigh.
I can see him hooray, hooray!

Tinsel covering all the house.
Nothing can be heard, not even a mouse.
All the children shout with glee
As they run and look at the Christmas tree.

Crackers being pulled with a *snap, snap, snap.*
I've got a toy that goes *zap!*
Bells are ringing, children are singing.
I think of all the toys Santa's bringing.

Stuffed with cake you will go to bed
And think of future that lies ahead.
Oh for all the joy Christmas can bring
All because of Christ, the newborn King.

That's Christmas!

Alice Byrne (9)
St Wilfrid's RCVA Primary School, Bishop Auckland

Epitaphs

Here lies the body
Of Goldilocks,
She was in bed
Because she had chickenpox.

Here lies the body
Of Sleeping Beauty
She thought apples
Were very fruity.

Here lies the body
Of Katie Price,
Got infected
By head lice.

Here lies the body
Of Tony Blair,
He thought he had
Fancy underwear.

Amy Biggins (9)
St Wilfrid's RCVA Primary School, Bishop Auckland

Buzzard

B ird of prey
U p it goes
Z any flying then
Z ooms below.
A ccurately the buzzard swoops down
R ats squealing
D inner found.

Daniel Igoe (8)
St Wilfrid's RCVA Primary School, Bishop Auckland

The Writer Of This Poem
(Inspired by 'The Writer Of This Poem' by Roger McGough)

Is as tall as a bus
is as keen as a blizzard
and always makes a fuss.

Is as soft as snow
as nimble as a sprite
is smaller than Tom Thumb.

As dark as night

As bright as the sun
As hard as a stone
As weak as a kitten
Is better than none.

Is faster than a whirlwind
As slow as a snail
As creepy as a spider
As empty as a pail.

Maryanne McLeavey (9)
St Wilfrid's RCVA Primary School, Bishop Auckland

My Mam

Mother's Day for you,
I love you too.
I love you, I love you so, so much,
I hope you have a great day on Mother's Day,
morning to night all the way,
I love you so much.

I know you are always on the phone
and sometimes you are alone,
I know you like cuddles,
and definitely poodles,
I love you so much.

Thank you for buying me presents,
thank you for loving me.
I know you like watching soaps,
like Emmerdale and Corrie,
I love you so much.

Tia Hinds (9)
St Wilfrid's RCVA Primary School, Bishop Auckland

My Special Mum

Mum thank you for loving me
Thank you for when you look after me
You are so special to me
When you do things for me.

Hope you have a great day
On Mother's Day morning.
Tonight I will do everything
You want me to do.

Thank you for making my tea
When I come in from school.
Thank you for my breakfast
Before I go to school.

Shannon Grady (8)
St Wilfrid's RCVA Primary School, Bishop Auckland

My Mam

You might be in the bath,
Or you might be phoning up your sister Cath,
But although you're 48,
You'll still be my best mate.

You might be eating your dinner,
Or you might be getting thinner,
But although you're sometimes a pain,
You'll never wake me with a cane.

Jessica Barker (9)
St Wilfrid's RCVA Primary School, Bishop Auckland

The Who's Who Of The Haunted House

Inside the
Horrible haunted house there is
An angry, aqua alligator attacking!
A beastly, bloodsucking bear bouncing!
A creepy, crazy crab crawling!
A dangerous, damaging dinosaur dying!
An energetic, elegant elephant eating!
A fearsome, fiery fairy flying!
A gigantic, gruesome gamekeeper galloping!
A hairy, horrible hairdresser hammering!
An incredible, icy insect impressing!
A jabbering, joyful jacket juggling!
A killing, kidnapping kangaroo kicking!
A lying, laughing ladybird landing!
A muddy, mad machine moving!
A nasty, neat nanny goat gnawing!
An Olympic ordering onion oinking!
A painful, paper penguin pushing!
A quirking queer queen quacking!
A racing, raging radio raining!
A scared, sneezing sacrifice saving!
A tacky, turning table touching!
An uncomfortable upside down uncle urging!
A valuable vanilla vegetable visiting!
A waddling, wicked weapon weeping!
A yapping, yellow yeti yelling!
A zipping, zigzag zebra zooming!
    That's all the things in the horrible, haunted house!

Helen Watson (9)
St Wilfrid's RCVA Primary School, Bishop Auckland

Yes It Is A Green Word

It grows like grass.
It's as crinkly as cabbage.
It's as lush as lime.
As springy as sprouts.
It's as lollopy as a lettuce.
As playful as peas.
As artistic as apples.
Yes it's as lazy as summer leaves.
It's even as squelchy as a fistful of lime.

Amy Ross (9)
St Wilfrid's RCVA Primary School, Bishop Auckland

Who'z Who Of The Haunted House

Inside the horrible house there is
an angry, aqua alligator attacking
a beastly, bloodsucking bear bouncing
a creepy, crazy crab crawling
a dangerous, damaging dinosaur dying
an energetic, evil elephant exercising
a frightened, fiery fly fighting
a gigantic, giggling ghost gazing
a harsh, huge horse hitting
an intelligent, indigo insect inspecting
a jumping, jolly juggler juggling
a knitting, kicking kangaroo killing
a laughing, limping leopard licking
a mad, making monkey marching
a naughty, nasty nephew nipping
an obedient, Olympic optician operating
a pale, particular panther partying
a quacking, queer queen quitting
a ragged, ravenous receiver recording
a sad, salty sausage swimming
a talented, tearful team telling
an ugly, unbelievable uncle understanding
a warm, wanted waiter waiting
a yellow, yapping yacht yawning
a zany, zappy zebra zooming.

Brogan McDonald (9)
St Wilfrid's RCVA Primary School, Bishop Auckland

The Writer Of This Poem
(Based on 'The Writer Of This Poem' by Roger McGough)

The writer of this poem
Is as tall as a tree,
The writer of this poem
Happens to be me.

The writer of this poem
Is as fast as a fish,
As swift as the wind,
As strong as an ox,
As sly as a fox.

The writer of this poem
Is as happy as can be,
As smart as a dolphin plunging in the sea.

The writer of this poem
Is as brave as a soldier marching along,
As sweet as a bird
Singing a song.

Catherine Clarke (9)
St Wilfrid's RCVA Primary School, Bishop Auckland

The Night

The skyscraper's standing tall
Like a soldier ready for war,
They climb the night,
Like a ladder going high.

The stars sparkling through the night
Lighting up the dark
Like twinkling lights.

Those down there
Can feel the cool breeze
Of the night
Settling down across their cheeks.

Beth Crossan (11)
Wingate Junior School

Tropical Breeze!

See the rainbow bursting through the mist
See the trees blowing in the wind
See the water running in a race.

Smell the air hovering around you
Smell the pollen floating away from tropical flowers
Smell the mist arising from the deep
Smell the dry leaves as they float to safety.

Hear the crashing of the waterfall
Hear the twittering of the birds high up in the trees
Hear the rustling trees, as they huddle up together.

Taste the water arising up to you
Taste the air that floats to you
Taste the damp moss that's under your feet.

Touch the whistling wind passing through your fingertips
Touch the leaves as they lay in your path
Touch the water that trickles through your hand.

As I sit on the mountain the tropical breeze cools me
And I feel relaxed.

Gina Parkin (11)
Wingate Junior School

Walt Disney

Minnie, Mickey,
Piglet, Pooh,
Eeyore, Tigger,
They all love you.
Fox and hound best friend
But why?
Trust me, they make you cry.
Walt Disney, he made them up,
He made a store,
How horrible!
He sells them on a cup.

Sarah Dinsdale (9)
Wingate Junior School

Witches' Storm

I heard the never-ending thunder crashing,
I constantly saw the lightning flashing.

Peeping outside, seeing the torrential rain,
Tasting of salt, all simple and plain.

I had a vision of a witch's finger,
As I opened my eyes, I saw it linger.

They tried to grab the helpless Earth's crust,
I looked carefully and saw particles of dust.

I faintly heard the crash of thunder,
While the rest of the world was left to wonder.

Helen Carter (11)
Wingate Junior School

The Mountain Animals

As the animals hear
The sound of water
They creep out of the trees
Gasping for a drink.

The clear sky
Makes them happy
Because they know
They are safe on the mountain.

As they travel back
They have some fruit
Juicy as can be
Before they sleep.

As the rainbow
Travels over the sky
The animals see a beautiful sight
Before it becomes night.

Christopher Wright (10)
Wingate Junior School

Silinder Alley

In the streets of Silinder Alley
On a dark, gloomy night,
A shining, silver coin
Lights the ancient weathered trees,
Beside a crooked fence.
But alas,
Peace and silence of the white covers
Laying among the streets
Is shattered
By a cry of moaning
Howled across for many hours.
Until little drops of ice
Float down,
Gently masking everything
They touch.

Emma Jones (11)
Wingate Junior School

Lightning

As I attack the undamaged buildings,
I am left to look at the remains,
As I strike, I listen to the sound of *boom!*
I sprint towards the trees and leave them burning,
I can smell thick, black smoke
And not long after, I can taste the smoke.
When I miss my target
And hit the hard, gravely road,
I can feel the shock up through my body,
I feel sorry for everything I've done,
But I know I'll do it all again in the next storm.
I can't hold it,
It's my nature . . .

Peter Clish (11)
Wingate Junior School

A Snowy Night

Peeping through the darkness
Bringing up the alley
Reflections of the snow
Illuminates all the branches on the trees
Silver moonlight falls across the land.

A hazy mist
Hanging like crystals
Falling to the ground
It makes a soft, white blanket
Delicate snowflakes floating across the land.

Robert Moore (11)
Wingate Junior School

I Want To Be . . .

I want to be a pop star
And have a posh sports car
I want to be
The pop star I see.

I want to be a beauty queen
To be fabulous and always seen
I want to be
The dream I wish to be.

I want to be a teacher
To make and learn
And play games with children
And let them take their turn.

I want to be
Just normal, little, me!

Olivia Moran (9)
Wingate Junior School

Pets

My pet is a dog
He waggles his tail
My pet is a dog
He barks like a whale.

I have a guinea pig
I had some toads too
We all lived in harmony and played together
Like me and you do.

I like my pets
I will never give them away
I like my pets
I will never lead them astray.

Connor Wilkinson (9)
Wingate Junior School

I Am A Roman Soldier

I am a Roman soldier
Plodding in the cold
I'll never leave the army
Even when I'm old.

We built the wall to save us all
The Celts are in sight
We draw our swords
We are prepared to fight.

Thomas McGlen (9)
Wingate Junior School

A Recipe For A Rainbow

A ring of red rubies
An arch of oranges
A streak of yellow sunset
A field of lush, green grass
A stream of blue
A smear of indigo dust
A bunch of violet pansies
Add a sprinkle of rain
And a splash of sunshine
Then mix them together
To make the greatest
Rainbow ever!

Hayley Davison (11)
Wingate Junior School

I Want To Be . . .

I want to be a fireman
Putting out a fire.
I want to be a hobbit
Working in the Shire.

I want to be a woodcutter
Cutting down a tree.
I want to be an Italian
Eating spaghetti.

I want to be an Indian
Eating tandoori.
I want to be in Nemo
Playing Dori.

I want to be,
I want to be,
I want to be,
Just like me!

Sam Forster (8)
Wingate Junior School

Pig

Trough cleaner
Mouth dribbler
Mud roller
Sunbather
Hay warmer
Trot clopper
Bacon giver!

Amy Cowey (11)
Wingate Junior School

My Mum

I love my mum
Till my days end
I love my mum
Even though I drive her round the bend.

She doesn't make my bed
She looks after the dog instead.

My mum buys me a lot of stuff
Although she can be tough.

She cooks my food
She is always in a mood.

My mum hoovers the floor
And always slams the door.

But

I love my mum
Till my days end
I love my mum
Even though I drive her round the bend.

Kieran Robson (9)
Wingate Junior School

Cars

Back firing
Dark lighting
Rubber burning
Cars turning
Petrol sucking
Gear changing
Street racing
Music blazing
Fast learning
Tyres burning.

Craig Turnbull (10)
Wingate Junior School

Cold Places

C old
O r snowing
L ong days
D ays are cold

P laying in the snow
L ong, cold nights
A very, cold place
C old all the time
E very day you wear thick clothes
S nowy places.

Danielle Rankin (10)
Wingate Junior School

Sandy Desert

S un
A nimals
N ot much water
D onkeys go for water
Y oung kids on their backs

D ark houses made from cliffs
E veryone climbs the mountains
S andy feet
E very day it has golden sand
R ed-hot weather
T rees sway in the breeze.

Chelsea Rowe (10)
Wingate Junior School

The Monster

I have a friend
He's a frog on one end
And a lion on the other half.

He helps me on sports day
By jumping away
To the finishing line.

He will bite off your foot
If under the table he's put
He really can be fierce.

But now he lives under the stairs
And everyday I comb his hair
He is a very good friend.

Liam Laverick (10)
Wingate Junior School

Winter

Winter is like a falling leaf
Lands on the earth like a soft blanket
It rushes around like a rampaging rhino
Covering everything in its path.

The little creatures hide from the raging beast
They gather there before the beast gets it
And leave the beast to starve.

It's time for the beast to leave
And start a new life.

James Blakelock (11)
Wingate Junior School

SATs

Everyone is down today
I really hope it's going to be OK.
I wish I just could skip them
And use my flying wings.
Then go somewhere that's really sunny
Above the clouds I go
To have a few words with myself
And I say
Please Mr Manager
Make them easy
Give me a level 5A
You'll be a real good star to me
But we all know now
You can't do that
So for goodness sake
Make them easy
Just when it comes to the English
I sweat through my vest
Then everyone make fun of me
So please be a good marker
Today!

Sophie Gilroy (11)
Wingate Junior School

My Mum

My fabulous mum
Is so much fun
Takes care of me
Read on and see
My mum is the best
She always cleans my stuff
Sometimes is a pest
And always is tough
She pulls me out of bed
And sometimes hurts my head
She puts me into bed at night
And puts off the light
My mum makes my dad a cup of tea
And always looks after me
She brings me a drink
And washes it in the sink
My fabulous mum
Is so much fun
Takes care of me
Read again and see.

John Dowson (8)
Wingate Junior School

I Want To Be . . .

I want to be a groovychick girl
You'd get to ride in a limo
I want to be a groovychick girl
I will clap and swirl.

I want to be a pop star
I will dance and sing and clap
I want to be a pop star
And I will dance on my dance mat.

I want to play the violin
It really is funny
I want to play a great big drum
And bang loud like a gun.

I want to be a swimmer
I really want to learn
I want to be a swimmer
And do a tumble turn.

Kaycee Donnelly (8)
Wingate Junior School

Nursery Rhyme

Humpty Dumpty sat on the wall
Eating red bananas
Then he died, fell off the wall and splattered all over the king
The king went berserk, fell off his horse
The horse ran off, back to the castle
On the bridge across the moat and into the castle
The king had to walk to the castle
When he got to the castle.

Ben Harris (8)
Wingate Junior School

My Polar Bear

My polar bear wets the bed
He cuddles his ted
Every night in the moonlight
He likes the night
He goes out into the street
He never eats his meat
My polar bear is fat
He likes his cat
He never makes a bang
He is too big to make a bang
My polar bear is good
He always is fast
He always catches his hat
He is a good guy
To help people over the road to safety
Especially old ladies across the street.

Sarah Owens (10)
Wingate Junior School

My Dog

My dog is bright
And can fight
And also it can write.
It can speak
And also think
Why he is licking his feet.
He likes peaches
And hates peas
And he also likes feet.

Carl Moyle (10)
Wingate Junior School

My Dog

My dog plays with the bony frogs
And the frogs play with the bony dog
And my dog growls and starts a toy fight.

My dog likes football
And always scores a goal
Because it takes the ball away in its mouth.

Wayne Bryson (11)
Wingate Junior School

I Am Going On Holiday

I am going on holiday
I am going in the car
I am going to the airport to catch a plane
When I am on holiday
I'll go on mini golf
And I might get a par.

When I am on the plane
I will be so high
I might meet a Great Dane
I will be able to see the aeroplane
Back in the sky.

I am on holiday
I am in Scotland
I am on holiday in my hotel
There's a place in Scotland called Totland
I suppose it is for tots.

I am going on holiday
I am going in the car
I am going to the airport to catch a plane
When I am on holiday
I'll go on mini golf
And I might get a par.

Daniel Cowey (8)
Wingate Junior School

What I Want To Be . . .

I want to be a doctor
And work with Mister Proctor.

I want to be an animal carer
And care for all the animals.

I want to be a woodcutter
Chopping up some wood.

I want to be . . .
I want to be . . .
I want to be . . .
I want to be me!

Lauren Smith (8)
Wingate Junior School

I Want To Be . . .

I want to be a pop star
I'd like to sing and dance
I want to be a pop star
I would like to have a chance.

I'd like to be a pop star
I think it's really great
I'll drive in my new sports car
And stay up really late.

I would like to be posh
I'd like to have some clothes
I'd like to have a lot of dosh
I would like a designer to paint my toes.

Ellie High (9)
Wingate Junior School

The Fairy

There was a beautiful fairy
Who had a little canary
She was all alone
She had a little home.

She was playing her game
But she kept on changing the ways
She was really nice
And she ate all the rice.

She went to play in the park
She couldn't find her way because it was dark
She went in the woods
It started to rain but she left her hood.

She was small
But she saw someone tall
She went to someone's house
And she found a little mouse.

Kimberley Roache (8)
Wingate Junior School

Daisy

D aily water the daisies
A ll the time there is a little daisy growing
I nto the grass the daisy grows
S nowy white
Y ellow middle.

Brittany Shaw (10)
Wingate Junior School

My Dog

My dog
Likes his frog
He even talks
But only for his walks
He's very cute
And loves his fruit.

Oranges, apples, bananas
He hides in my pyjamas
My dog's a sneaky thing
And gets a shock
When his tail goes ping
Now it's late
So me and my mate
Dressed in red
Go to bed!

Rebecca Leonard (10)
Wingate Junior School

Australia

Ozzy Australia what do you do?
I hear you in England we lay the didgeridoo
Ozzy Australia what do you play?
England we play with the best of things
Like boomerangs to the end of the day
Ozzy Australia I'm going now
Send me a postcard of what your town's like.

Jordan Hall (10)
Wingate Junior School

Jungle In Greece

J umping monkeys swinging on vines
U p and down slithering ivy
N ear death, here comes a sneaking python
G reek soldiers in armour ready to fight
L ending a spear to stab
E veryday luck

I n the jungle here come leopards
N ow fierce jaguars come to fight

G reeks in shining armour
R eally the country has spiders
E ven some toxic snakes
E velyn a princess clean
C lean as can be
E x, ex, a big rex.

Liam Hanson (9)
Wingate Junior School

Hollywood

H olding stars
O rdering stars around
L oving members
L aunching films
Y our place to go on holiday
W orld winners for awards
O ld films filming on the set
O pening scenes
D ollars to be spent.

Martin Mason (9)
Wingate Junior School

Cars

C ars are good when they have turbo
A nd they are even better when they have spray
R acing cars go fast in the race
S o you could get one if you have the money.

Nathan Goundry (9)
Wingate Junior School

A Day In The Life Of Me

Night fright
Darkness sight
Comb hair
Get to sleep
Bed warm
Count sheep
Deep sleep
Rise and shine
Breakfast time
Mum fusses
School buses
Open window
Half-three
Time for tea
Play in park
Until dark
Put bike away
Have a bath
Get my juice and supper
Go to bed
Watch TV
Go to sleep.

Erin Bellig (8)
Wingate Junior School

The Fairground

I am rushing round
The fairground
Wanting to get on
My favourite ride
Which is the slide
Jumping up and down
Like that silly, old clown.

When I am on the big wheel
I can see the seal
In the zoo doing tricks
For me and you.

When I am on the ghost train
I see a ghost plane
Coming out
I see the skeleton shout.

Going home in the car
I see that we are going far
Away from the ground
And then I hear a sound . . .

Sasha Louise Darby (11)
Wingate Junior School

Nursery Rhyme

What is the point in having a cat called Pat
On the mat, if you haven't got a rat.
A cat can chase a rat under the mat
If you have a rat, what's the point in having a cat
On the mat if you haven't got a rat.
So, if you have a pet rat, you'd better watch out
For the cat on the mat.

Jennifer Coulson (8)
Wingate Junior School

A Lurcher

My cousin has a lurcher
Which hunts around all day.
It glides around the water
And dives around the hay.

That dog is always hungry
She runs fast, I don't know how
If she ever escaped from the garden
She would try to eat a cow!

Luke Hanlon (11)
Wingate Junior School

Autumn

Autumn came
And we saw the rain
From the cloud,
Then aloud.
There my mother stood
When she saw her trousers clean,
Then five minutes later,
We saw some steam,
So we went outside
And soon the rain stopped
And my guinea pig hopped
Then jumped to the top.

Craig Taylor (9)
Wingate Junior School

Monster

There's a monster under my bed
What will I do?

Maybe he is friendly
And would like to come to the zoo?

Or perhaps he is hungry
And wants to eat me up?

He might be cuddly
Like a newborn pup!

Sarah Hall (11)
Wingate Junior School

A Day In The Life Of A Football Supporter

Daytime
Daytime
Cereal time
Time to go
Football starts
Finished half
Getting started
Second half
Finished game
Go home
Time for bed
Warmness
Time to sleep
Count sheep
Deep sleep
Have a dream
Wake up late
Have a drink
Go back to sleep
Getting warm
Counting sheep.

Jack Deluce (8)
Wingate Junior School

Dog

My dog is a mutt
He eats all the time
He is very cuddly
We always take him for walks
He plays until we go in the house
Then he cries when he jumps up at the window
That's because we don't play with him
All the time.

Kayleigh Renwick (10)
Wingate Junior School

I Can . . .

I can skip
I can do work
I can do tests
I can play football
I can play games
I can play with a hula hoop in the yard
I can jump in hay
I can ride a horse
I can do loads of hops
I can ride a bike
I can play with a dog!

Can you ride a bike?
Can you do work?
Can you do tests?
Can you jump in hay?
Can you skip?
Can you ride a horse?
Can you do loads of hops?
Can you play football?
Can you play with a hula hoop in the yard?
Can you play with a dog?

Clare Armstrong (7)
Wingate Junior School

I Had A Pet

I had a pet called Harry,
He was easy to carry.
I had a goldfish,
It wasn't a very bold fish.
Now I have two cats,
They don't look like bats,
But they certainly do eat rats!

Joshua Adam Hare (8)
Wingate Junior School

Pets

Monday . . . My dog jumped onto the table.
　　　　　　My bird fell into the fish tank.
　　　　　　The fish jumped out of the fish tank.
　　　　　　And got stuck on the sticky label.

Tuesday . . . My cat fell off the roof
　　　　　　My hamster fell in the sink
　　　　　　Then my parrot started to tell the truth
　　　　　　And the dog started to drink.

Wednesday . . . My guinea pig wouldn't eat
　　　　　　My mouse ate all the cake
　　　　　　The sheep started to bleat
　　　　　　Then the snake started to bake.

Mathew Tuttle (8)
Wingate Junior School

Spring

Spring is nice when it is hot
Pretty flowers appear today
Running creatures run all day
Ice cream cold to keep us cool
Nice day, stay all day and play
Great to see me and my friends
Splashing about in the pool
Sometimes we read books that are great.

Jade Addison (10)
Wingate Junior School

Deserts

Lying in the calm desert breeze,
The sand is really making me sneeze.

Hard at work, digging for food,
My sister is in a really bad mood.

Cacti standing in the desert sun,
I am eating a ruby-red bun.

Eating up my apply pie,
Deserts are hot, sunny, sandy and dry.

Chelsea McCann (10)
Wingate Junior School

Forest

F or brave people
O r strong people
R ivers all around you
E mpty
S cary things
T rees weaving around you.

Rajvir Gill (10)
Wingate Junior School

The Viking Who Went Hiking

There once was a Viking,
Who decided one day, to go hiking.
As he climbed the mountain,
He discovered a large fountain.

The poor Viking looked straight into it
He saw an Inuit.
The poor thing started to cry,
Then poked the Viking in the eye!

James Hughes (10)
Wingate Junior School

Desert

D eserted lands
E verything almost dead
S unny all the time
E vening temperature drops below zero
R ainwater falls underground
T o get water, need to dig far underground.

Stacey Marriott (10)
Wingate Junior School

Penguins

P enguins live near the sea in very cold places
E very kind, all different sizes
N ear the sea, they play
G liding on their bellies
U nder the ice, they swim
I n spring
N ew babies
S liding down the hills.

Marley Donnelly (10)
Wingate Junior School

The Sheep Pig

There once was a pig
He could not dig
Elephants would laugh at him
Sheep pig was next, he tried
But looked really dim.
He asked the sheep
If he could round them all up
Evil wolves would chase us
And put us in a cup.
Everything went well at first
People started to cheer and burst
Pig was no longer alone
Instead he would not groan
He now has a fantastic tone.

Maryanne Jackson (10)
Wingate Junior School

Flowers

F lowers growing in the bright, blue sky
L ong stems
O ther flowers getting watered
W atering them on and on
E ven flowers swirl around
R unning around after them.

Amy Fulton (10)
Wingate Junior School

My Mum

My super mum
Takes care of me
My super mum
Makes me a cup of tea.

My mum cooks for me
She makes me a lovely lunch
I dash to the shop
And buy her a lovely bunch.

My mum tidies my room
She puts my clothes away
My mum takes me places
It's a really sunny day.

My super mum
Takes care of me
My super mum
Makes me a cup of tea!

Sarah Cowey (9)
Wingate Junior School

Playtime

Shout out names
Play some games
What shall we play
On this bright, sunny day?
Let's play polo
Get down low.
Snakes and ladders are fun to play
Yes, I've won on this day.
Stuck in the mud?
I know I would.
Football coming
As I'm humming
Shout out names
Play some games.

Rebecca Dixon (9)
Wingate Junior School

Food

I like fruit
Maybe an orange
I like fruit
Always say *mmm* . . . orange.

I like sweets
Mmm chocolate
I like sweets
There's a sugar droplet.

I like dinner
Pudding are the best
I like dinner
Mum, I dropped it on my vest!

I like spaghetti
I have it with toast
I like spaghetti
I like it the most.

Chloe Davison (9)
Wingate Junior School

I'd Like To Be . . .

I'd like to be a pop star
I think it would be great
I'd like to be a pop star
And stay up to practise late.

Dad's in late, see him later on
Dad I need a hand
I want to be a rock star
And join a great big band.

I'd like to be
Mr Bean
He's the greatest
Ever seen.

I'd like to be
A Barbie girl
Stand on TV
Do a twirl.

I'd like to be
A doctor
And work with
Mr Foster.

Charlotte Unsworth (9)
Wingate Junior School

Undead Monster

There's a monster under my bed
The freakiest thing is, he's undead.
He jumps to the cupboard and hides all day,
But at night he comes out to play.
At dawn he runs away indoor
And slowly fades away.

David Wade (11)
Wingate Junior School

In The Deep, Dark Wood

In the deep, dark wood
I make something good
Like child pud
Put in some blood
And pour in some mud.

Andrew Nichol (7)
Wingate Junior School

In The Dark Woods

In the dark woods
There was a dead rat
That was very black
That had been killed
By another rat
A bat came
And ate the rat.

Heather Marriott (7)
Wingate Junior School

Untitled

Dogs are mad
Kittens are cute
Sometimes they are happy
Sometimes they are sad
Sometimes they are bad
And they chew everything
They always get on your nerves
They always want to play.

Danielle Ridden (9)
Wingate Junior School

Pets

The dogs are mad
And the fish are thin
The cats are sad
Now just dump them in the bin.
Look at the chickens
See that bunny
Look, there's kittens
So don't you think that's funny.
No the dog is dead
It ate the bunny
There it is, lying in the bed
Now give me some money.

Rebecca Bailey (9)
Wingate Junior School

Roman Soldier

I am a Roman
Fighting in battles
You are a lowman
We all ride cattle.

I steal lots of gold
We got in a fight
The beds are always cold
It is almost night.

We love to fight
We are not scared
No in the night
We never cared.

Reece Devonport (8)
Wingate Junior School

I Want To Be . . .

I want to be a rugby player
I would also like to be a pop star
And be rich with a very posh Jaguar car.

I want to be a fast runner
Going down the road
I would run the London Marathon
And walk all the way back
Because my medals weighed a tonne.

I want to be an actor
I would meet new friends
I won't forget my words
And the scenery never bends.

Jamie Robinson (8)
Wingate Junior School

I Want To Be . . .

I want to be a racing driver
I would win every race
It is better than being a diver
If you are a racing driver you earn lots of money.

I want to be a forensic scientist
I would find the murderer
We found the dead body in the mist
The murderer used a knife to kill them.

I want to be a ninja
I would stop the bad ninjas
The bad ninjas are whingers
In the night, bad ninjas chop people's heads off.

Alex Routledge (8)
Wingate Junior School

My Funny Family

First, there is Billy with his little dog Filly.
And then there is Dennis with his alley cat Menace.
My Auntie Norse has a ride on her horse.
Isabell the cow has to get milked now.
Lately Ginny has lost her rabbits Minny and Pinny
Yet I am the only one without something to do.

Danielle Robinson (10)
Wingate Junior School

A Day In The Life Of A Football Supporter

Play football everyday
Go to sleep, wake up, play football
And play football, never stop all day
Play football, score lots of goals
Never stop playing football all day
And play football for a team.
Go on the right side of midfield
Go in and sometimes I am a goalkeeper
Sometimes in defence and tackle
And sometimes in the middle of midfield
Sometimes up front, that means where you are in front
And when you are in goal, you have to save the shot
And you score lots and lots of goals.

Ryan Murphy (8)
Wingate Junior School

A Day In The Life Of A Football Player

Kick off
Football
Free kick
See Nick
See Rick
Offside
Pitch
Referee
Near me
Score no more
Full time
Every time
Team score
Crossbar far
Penalty injury
Mick is sick
Kick Nick
Kick Mick
Everybody goes wild
Header
Corner.

Gemma Robson (9)
Wingate Junior School

In A Deep, Dark Week

In a deep, dark week
The rats start charging
Where the flies go peep
Where the cows go barging
Where chimps start weeping
The horses start charging
The pigs start sweeping
Where everybody starts marching.

Lewis Coils (8)
Wingate Junior School

Untitled

Add one fly
Throw in a bee
A bit of blue dye
Then add a flea.

Add a fox
Throw in a long fish
One big box
Throw it in a dish.

Pour in some pop
Add one chair
Then make into a shop
Then put in a bear.

Karl Laverick (8)
Wingate Junior School

A Day In The Life Of Me

Day down
Stretch, yawn
Rise and shine
Morning rhyme
Breakfast time
No surprise
Queen flies
No surprise
Time flies
Half-three
Time for tea
In the park
Until dark
Quick, toilet
Then was
Time for bed
Bed warm
Count sheep
Deep sleep.

Callia Addison (7)
Wingate Junior School

Nonsense

Add in a nail
Put in some card
Or maybe a snail
Throw in some lard.

Put in some hair
Throw in some stones
Or an autograph from Tony Blair
And some ice cream cones.

Throw in a broom
Put in some metal
Add something from the room
Or a kettle.

Put in a fish
Toss in a pea
Throw them in a dish
And there you have it - your tea!

Amy Jill Kell (8)
Wingate Junior School

Ingredients

I add some pop
I put in some butter
To make it stop
To make it flutter.

Add in some butts
Here comes a fly
To make it nuts
To kill the blue dye.

A toss in a box
Get a chef
Plop in a fox
Add one leaf.

Jake Dowson (8)
Wingate Junior School

I Want To Be . . .

I want to be a superstar
And travel very far
I want to be a passport
And be a great sport.

I want to be a monkey
And be very funky
I want to be a pig
With a great big jig.

I want to be a pencil pot
With a great big spot
I want to be a motorbike
That's what I want to be.

I want to be a superstar
And travel very far
That's not what I want to be
I'm really happy as me.

Charlotte Patterson (7)
Wingate Junior School

Cars

C ars are fast and furious
A nd are very smart
R ush to places very fast
S ure, they have accelerators.

Liam Harris (9)
Wingate Junior School

School

S chool is cool
C ool in school because it has maths
H ot outside school
O n the schoolroom floor, you can eat off the floor
O n the playground is snakes and ladder
L ovely school is Wingate Junior School.

Chelsea Jeffery (10)
Wingate Junior School

Fairground Fun!

Dripping ice cream, monkey's blood,
Chopped nuts, yummy sweets,
Slurp, slurp, lots of treats.

On and on runs the water log
Dashing here, dashing there,
Dashing here, everywhere,
Water gushing in my face,
Speeding up at a faster pace!

Wind in my face, round the track,
Return to a tunnel, oh no! pitch black,
Back to the start I will go,
My tummy curdling, fingers trembling!

Ruby McGlen (11)
Wingate Junior School

The Mysterious Journey

The animals want the pot of gold
At the end of the rainbow
So the animals set
On their way
They met a man that said,
'When you get the gold,
Please will you give me some?'
The animals were wondering
How he could talk to them.

Paul Atkinson (11)
Wingate Junior School

I Want To Be A Pop Star

I want to be a pop star
I want to dance like Britney.
I want to drive a car
Can I be a solo singer?

It might be scary but I don't care
I might have a squeaky voice
I could be the mayor
I want to be a pop star.

I want to be a pop star
I want to be great
I want to be a pop star
And stay up really late.

I want to be a pop star
I want to dance like you
I want to be beautiful
I want to prance about too!

Rebecca Siddle (8)
Wingate Junior School

Friends

My friend is so silly
His name is Billy
His friend is Jay
And he has to pay.

My friend is Vinnie
And he does vodo villie
My friend is Ben
And he counts to ten.

My friend is Josh
And he thinks he's posh
My friend is Bess
And he's in a mess.

Dean Murrell (9)
Wingate Junior School

I Want To Be . . .

I want to be a pop star
Staying up really late
Being on the TV
And playing with my mates.

I want to be a fish
Swimming in the sea
Swimming round and round
And eating seaweed for my tea.

I want to be an angel
Making lots of wishes
Flying up in the air
And turning things into fishes.

I want to be a fairy
Making lots of spells
Wearing nice dresses
And having lots of shells.

I want to be myself
Playing a game
Riding my bike
I want to be the same.

Shannon Bracknell (8)
Wingate Junior School

I Want To Be A Pop Star

I want to be a pop star
And get a really cool car
I want to be a pop star
And sing in the light stars
When I wake up
I put on my make-up.

I want to be a pop star
And shop around town
I want to be a pop star
And have a gold crown.

I want to be a pop star
And have really good stuff
I want to be a pop star
I am really tough.

Laura Booth (9)
Wingate Junior School

My Family

My uncle has no hair
My auntie drives a car
My mam kissed Tony Blair
My uncle hangs around the bar
I doubt that was a dare.

Ryan Parkin (9)
Wingate Junior School

Ruthless Rules

Here are the rules you get in Grandma's house
Always be quiet
Make sure you don't step on Grandma's mouse
Do not start a riot.

Do not jump on her chairs
Do not touch her dog
Do not go racing down the stairs
Do not touch her log.

Jay Foster (9)
Wingate Junior School

Changing Colours

Pink is the classroom
With wallboards bright
Sees a child get a fright.

White is the child
Playing with glee
Sees a bird in a tree.

Black is the bird
With dark silver wings
Sees a girl with her favourite things.

Peach is the girl
With light brown hair
Sees a school standing there.

Stephanie Williams (11)
Wingate Junior School